THE COGNITIVE DEVELOPMENT - A NEW ERA

THE COGNITIVE DEVELOPMENT - A NEW ERA

Mahendra Jagir

Studio of Books LLC
5900 Balcones Drive Suite 100
Austin, Texas 78731
www.studioofbooks.org
Hotline: (254) 800-1183

Ordering Information:
Special discounts are available on quantity purchases by corporations, associations, and others. For details, contact the publisher at the address above.

Printed in the United States of America.

ISBN-13: Paperback   978-1-970283-34-1
         Ebook   978-1-970283-35-8

Library of Congress Control Number: 2026905201

Dedication

This book is dedicated to Dustin, Matthew, Georgia,and Jolie.

May this work become more than a book you read.

May it become a way of thinking.

The future is not shaped only by inventions, structures, or systems. It is shaped by the minds that understand them, protect them, and improve them.

One day, you may inherit responsibilities that go far beyond ordinary tasks. Among them are the SHIELD Project and the SAN, ideas created to strengthen communities, safeguard knowledge, and help build a better future.

But the most important inheritance is not the project itself.

The most important inheritance is the way of thinking required to guide it wisely.

To observe carefully.

To understand deeply.

To see connections others may overlook.

To think ahead before making decisions.

This book was written so that you—and all young learners—can develop the kind of mind that sees the world clearly and understands the systems that shape it.

Knowledge alone is not enough.

True leadership requires awareness, patience, and responsibility.

May you always remain curious about the world May you continue asking questions long after this book is finished.And may you remember that the greatest legacy we pass forward is not only what we build—but the ability to think clearly and guide the future wisely.

Preface

A New Way to Learn Before children learn to read books, they must first learn how to **read the world.**

Every single day, your eyes and mind collect information from the world around you. You see trees swaying gently in the wind. You notice birds flying across the sky. You watch cars moving through busy city streets and people working together in communities. At first, these may look like simple everyday moments. But if you look a little closer, you will discover that each moment is part of a much bigger story.

The world is full of **systems.**

A system is when many parts work together to make something function. Sometimes we do not notice systems right away because they are happening all around us at the same time.

For example, a **forest** is a system. Trees grow together with plants, insects, animals, soil, sunlight, and water. Each part depends on the others. When rain falls, plants grow. When plants grow, animals have food and shelter. When animals move through the forest, they spread seeds that help new plants grow. Everything is connected.

A **city** is also a system. Roads allow cars and buses to travel. Buildings provide places for people to live and work. Electricity powers lights and machines. Water flows through pipes so people can cook, clean, and drink. Thousands of people cooperate to keep a city running every day.

Even a **school** is a system. Teachers guide learning, students ask questions, books provide knowledge, and classrooms create spaces where ideas can grow. Everyone plays a role in helping the system work well.

Families and communities are systems too. People support one another, share responsibilities, and help solve problems together.

When you begin to understand systems, something exciting happens. You start to notice how actions create results. If one part of a system changes, other parts are affected as well. A small change can sometimes lead to a big result.

This book introduces a powerful idea: **Understanding should come before memorizing words.**

Many traditional ways of learning begin with reading letters, sounding out words, and memorizing sentences. Those skills are important, but strong thinking begins even earlier. Before children fully read books, they already have the ability to **observe, wonder,** and **think about what they see.**

When children learn to carefully observe the world around them, their thinking becomes stronger and more flexible. Observation trains the brain in many important ways. It helps develop:

- Memory
- Critical thinking
- Patience
- Problem-solving skills
- Ethical reasoning

Observation also encourages curiosity. When children look closely at the world, they begin asking powerful questions.

Why does this happen?

What caused it?

What might happen next?

These questions are the starting point of intelligent thinking. Many discoveries, inventions, and ideas began with someone simply noticing something interesting and asking a thoughtful question.

In this book, you will explore **twenty real-world scenes**. Each scene is like a window into a different system in the world. Some scenes may show nature, others may show cities or communities, and some may show people working together.

Your job is not just to look at the pictures. Your job is to **think about them.**

As you explore each scene, you will practice important thinking skills such as:

- Identifying relationships between people, objects, and events
- Predicting what might happen next
- Understanding emotions and themes in situations
- Thinking about long-term consequences of actions

These skills help your brain grow stronger every time you practice them.

The goal of this book is not only to help you succeed in school. The goal is to help you develop the kinds of thinking skills that will guide you throughout your entire life.

One day, today's young learners will grow into adults who build the future. Some may become engineers who design bridges and machines. Others may become scientists who study nature and discover new knowledge. Some may become teachers who guide the next generation of learners. Others may become builders, artists, leaders, doctors, farmers, inventors, or caretakers of communities.

No matter which path someone chooses, the ability to **understand complex systems** will always be valuable. It helps people solve problems, work together, and make thoughtful decisions that improve the world around them.

This is why the ideas in this book are part of a larger concept called **Legacy Learning.**

Legacy learning means preparing the next generation not only to inherit knowledge, but also to inherit the **thinking skills needed to guide the future responsibly.**

When you strengthen your ability to observe, question, and understand systems today, you are building tools that will help you shape tomorrow.

And every great journey of learning begins with something very simple:

Learning to see clearly.

Table of Contents

How to Use This Book

(For Parents, Teachers, and Young Readers)

This book is designed to help children develop strong thinking skills by learning to observe, analyze, and understand the world visually before focusing mainly on written text. Instead of beginning with long explanations or memorized facts, this book invites readers to start with what children naturally do best: look, notice, wonder, and think.

The scenes and exercises throughout this book are meant to encourage curiosity, reflection, conversation, and thoughtful decision-making. Each part of the book helps children strengthen their ability to pay attention to details, identify patterns, predict outcomes, and think about how actions affect the world around them.

This is not a book that should be rushed.

It is a book to explore slowly.

It is a book to return to.

It is a book that asks the reader to pause, look closely, and think deeply.

Children are often naturally curious about their surroundings. They notice movements, sounds, colors, changes in weather, facial expressions, and patterns in everyday life. This book builds on that natural curiosity and helps transform it into stronger habits of reasoning, comprehension, and ethical awareness.

At its heart, this book teaches children to do something powerful:

to read the world before reading words.

That means learning how to look at a scene and ask thoughtful questions:

- What do I notice?

- What might happen next?

- How are these things connected?

- How do people, animals, objects, and environments affect one another?

- What choices in this situation are helpful, harmful, fair, or responsible?

These questions strengthen the mind in ways that go far beyond one subject or one classroom. They help children become better thinkers in all parts of life.

For Children

As you explore the scenes in this book, remember that this is not a race. You do not need to hurry.

Each scene is like a puzzle, a story, and a lesson all at the same time. The more carefully you look, the more you will discover.

Here are a few helpful ways to approach each scene:

Take your time observing each image carefully.

Some details in a scene are easy to notice right away. Others are smaller, quieter, or hidden in the background. When you slow down and look closely, you begin to see much more than you noticed at first glance.

A person rushing past a scene might only notice the biggest objects. But a thoughtful observer notices the little things too—the direction of the wind, the expression on a person's face, the way one object is affecting another, or how people and animals share the same space.

Notice small details that others might miss.

The small details often matter the most.

A broken swing on a playground may change how children move. A dark cloud over a boat may suggest changing weather. A bird sitting quietly near a tree may show that the environment is calm and safe.

Sometimes one tiny detail can reveal an important clue.

Ask yourself questions about what might be happening.

Learning becomes stronger when you become curious.

Do not be afraid to wonder. Ask yourself questions such as:

- Why is that happening?
- What caused this?
- What are the people in the scene doing?
- Are they working together?
- Is something changing?
- What might happen next?

Questions are not signs that you do not know enough. Questions are signs that your mind is active and growing.

Imagine what could happen next.

A strong thinker does not only describe what is happening now. A strong thinker also begins to imagine possible outcomes.

This helps build foresight, which means thinking ahead.

If rain begins, what changes in the scene?

If an object moves, who is affected?

If someone makes a helpful or harmful choice, what might happen afterward?

These kinds of questions train your brain to connect observation with reasoning.

Think about how the people, animals, or objects in the scene are connected.

Very often, the world is not made of separate parts. It is made of relationships.

Trees provide shade.

Water helps plants grow.

Roads guide traffic.

Teachers help students learn.

Rules help people stay safe.

Animals depend on their habitats.

Communities depend on cooperation.
When you begin noticing these relationships, you are learning how systems work.

There are no "wrong" answers when you are thinking deeply and honestly.

Many children worry that they must always find one perfect answer. But this book is different.

The goal is not simply to be "right."

The goal is to learn how to **think well**.

Sometimes different readers may notice different details, ask different questions, or imagine different possibilities. That is part of learning. Good thinking often includes discussion, reflection, and seeing a situation from more than one point of view.

This book is here to help you train your mind to become more observant, more thoughtful, and more creative.

For Parents and Teachers

Parents, teachers, and caregivers play an important role in helping children develop the habits this book encourages. Although children can enjoy the scenes independently, the book becomes even more powerful when adults help turn visual observation into meaningful conversation.

Children not only learn from what they see. They also learn from what they are asked to think about.

When adults guide discussion with curiosity and patience, they help children move beyond simple description into deeper understanding.

You can support children's learning in several ways.

Encourage conversation, not just answers.

Instead of asking only whether a child got the "correct" answer, invite them to explain what they noticed and why they think it matters.

A scene becomes much more valuable when a child talks through their thinking.

For example, instead of saying, "That's right," you might ask:

- What made you notice that?
- What clue helped you think that?
- What else could be happening?
- How might this change later?

These questions help children strengthen their reasoning and communication at the same time.

Ask open-ended questions.

Open-ended questions encourage children to think more deeply and consider more than one possibility.

- Helpful questions include:
- What do you notice first in this scene?
- What might happen next?
- Why do you think that?
- How do the different parts of the scene work together?
- What choices could the people in the scene make?
- Who might be helped by this action?
- Who might be affected if something changes?
- What details tell you this place is calm, busy, safe, or risky?

Questions like these encourage children to connect **observation, cause and effect, emotion, and ethical reflection.**

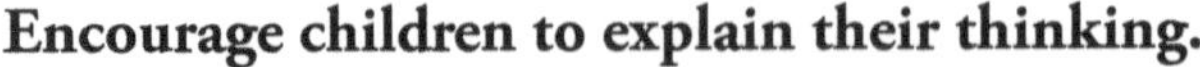

Encourage children to explain their thinking.

It is valuable for children to describe not only *what* they see, but also *how* they reached their conclusions.

This strengthens:

- attention
- memory
- verbal reasoning
- confidence
- self-awareness

It also helps adults better understand how the child is thinking, which can guide support and discussion more effectively.

Make room for different perspectives.

Two children may notice different things in the same scene. One child may focus on people. Another may focus on weather, animals, or movement.

This is not a problem. It is an opportunity.
By inviting children to listen to different observations, adults help them understand that complex situations can be viewed in multiple ways. This supports social learning, empathy, and flexible thinking.

Focus on habits of mind, not memorization.

The purpose of this book is not to have children memorize facts about scenes. The purpose is to help them develop strong habits of mind that support learning in every subject and throughout life.

These habits include:

- looking carefully
- asking thoughtful questions
- noticing relationships
- making predictions
- considering consequences
- thinking ethically
- reflecting before acting

These are life skills as much as academic skills.

A Note About Pace and Progress

Children do not all think in exactly the same way or at the same speed. Some may notice many details quickly. Others may need more time to feel confident sharing their observations. Some may enjoy prediction. Others may be especially interested in emotional or ethical questions.

That is perfectly normal.

This book is not meant to force one type of thinking. It is meant to strengthen thinking in a gradual, supportive, and engaging way.

Adults should feel free to:

- revisit scenes

- continue conversations over multiple days

- connect scenes to real-life experiences

- adapt questions to the age and maturity of the child

The book can be used in classrooms, homeschool settings, tutoring sessions, family discussion time, or individual reflection.

What This Book Is Really Teaching

Although the scenes may appear simple at first, the deeper purpose of the book is much bigger.
- This book helps children learn how to:
- observe the world carefully
- think critically about what they see
- understand systems and relationships
- make responsible choices
- Imagine how the future can be shaped by actions today

These are powerful foundations not just for school success, but for life.

When children become strong observers, they also become stronger readers, better problem-solvers, better listeners, and more thoughtful members of their communities.

That is why this book begins with vision, curiosity, and reflection.

Before children learn to read many words, they can begin learning how to read **patterns, systems, relationships, and meaning**.

And that kind of learning can shape the rest of their lives.

The Cognitive Ladder Method

This book is designed to help children develop strong thinking skills by learning to observe, analyze, and understand the world visually before focusing mainly on written text. Instead of beginning with long explanations or memorized facts, this book invites readers to start with what children naturally do best: **look, notice, wonder, and think**.

The scenes and exercises throughout this book are meant to encourage curiosity, reflection, conversation, and thoughtful decision-making. Each part of the book helps children strengthen their ability to pay attention to details, identify patterns, predict outcomes, and think about how actions affect the world around them.

This is not a book that should be rushed.

It is a book to explore slowly.

It is a book to return to.

It is a book that asks the reader to pause, look closely, and think deeply.

Children are often naturally curious about their surroundings. They notice movements, sounds, colors, changes in weather, facial expressions, and patterns in everyday life. This book builds on that natural curiosity and helps transform it into stronger habits of reasoning, comprehension, and ethical awareness.

At its heart, this book teaches children to do something powerful:

to read the world before reading words.

That means learning how to look at a scene and ask thoughtful questions:

- What do I notice?
- What might happen next?

- How are these things connected?
- How do people, animals, objects, and environments affect one another?
- What choices in this situation are helpful, harmful, fair, or responsible?

These questions strengthen the mind in ways that go far beyond one subject or one classroom. They help children become better thinkers in all parts of life.

For Children

As you explore the scenes in this book, remember that this is not a race. You do not need to hurry.

Each scene is like a puzzle, a story, and a lesson all at the same time. The more carefully you look, the more you will discover.

Here are a few helpful ways to approach each scene:

Take your time observing each image carefully.

Some details in a scene are easy to notice right away. Others are smaller, quieter, or hidden in the background. When you slow down and look closely, you begin to see much more than you noticed at first glance.

A person rushing past a scene might only notice the biggest objects. But a thoughtful observer notices the little things too—the direction of the wind, the expression on a person's face, the way one object is affecting another, or how people and animals share the same space.

Notice small details that others might miss.

The small details often matter the most.

A broken swing on a playground may change how children move. A dark cloud over a boat may suggest changing weather. A bird sitting quietly near a tree may show that the environment is calm and safe.

Sometimes one tiny detail can reveal an important clue.

Ask yourself questions about what might be happening.

Learning becomes stronger when you become curious.

Do not be afraid to wonder. Ask yourself questions such as:

- Why is that happening?
- What caused this?

- What are the people in the scene doing?
- Are they working together?
- Is something changing?
- What might happen next?

Questions are not signs that you do not know enough. Questions are signs that your mind is active and growing.

Imagine what could happen next.

A strong thinker does not only describe what is happening now. A strong thinker also begins to imagine possible outcomes.

This helps build foresight, which means thinking ahead.

If rain begins, what changes in the scene?

If an object moves, who is affected?

If someone makes a helpful or harmful choice, what might happen afterward?

These kinds of questions train your brain to connect observation with reasoning.

Think about how the people, animals, or objects in the scene are connected.

Very often, the world is not made of separate parts. It is made of relationships.

Trees provide shade.

Water helps plants grow.

Roads guide traffic.

Teachers help students learn.

Rules help people stay safe.

Animals depend on their habitats.

Communities depend on cooperation.

When you begin noticing these relationships, you are learning how systems work.

There are no "wrong" answers when you are thinking deeply and honestly.

Many children worry that they must always find one perfect answer. But this book is different.

The goal is not simply to be "right."

The goal is to learn how to **think well**.

Sometimes different readers may notice different details, ask different questions, or imagine different possibilities. That is part of learning. Good thinking often includes discussion, reflection, and seeing a situation from more than one point of view.
This book is here to help you train your mind to become more observant, more thoughtful, and more creative.

For Parents and Teachers

Parents, teachers, and caregivers play an important role in helping children develop the habits this book encourages. Although children can enjoy the scenes independently, the book becomes even more powerful when adults help turn visual observation into meaningful conversation.

Children do not only learn from what they see. They also learn from what they are asked to think about.

When adults guide discussion with curiosity and patience, they help children move beyond simple description into deeper understanding.

You can support children's learning in several ways.

Encourage conversation, not just answers.

Instead of asking only whether a child got the "correct" answer, invite them to explain what they noticed and why they think it matters.

A scene becomes much more valuable when a child talks through their thinking.

For example, instead of saying, "That's right," you might ask:

- What made you notice that?
- What clue helped you think that?
- What else could be happening?
- How might this change later?

These questions help children strengthen reasoning and communication at the same time.

Ask open-ended questions.

Open-ended questions encourage children to think more deeply and consider more than one possibility.
Helpful questions include:

- What do you notice first in this scene?

- What might happen next?

- Why do you think that?

- How do the different parts of the scene work together?

- What choices could the people in the scene make?

- Who might be helped by this action?

- Who might be affected if something changes?

- What details tell you this place is calm, busy, safe, or risky?

Questions like these encourage children to connect **observation, cause and effect, emotion, and ethical reflection**.

Encourage children to explain their thinking.

It is valuable for children to describe not only *what* they see, but also *how* they reached their conclusions.

- This strengthens:
- attention
- memory
- verbal reasoning
- confidence
- self-awareness

It also helps adults better understand how the child is thinking, which can guide support and discussion more effectively.

Make room for different perspectives.

Two children may notice different things in the same scene. One child may focus on people. Another may focus on weather, animals, or movement.

This is not a problem. It is an opportunity.

By inviting children to listen to different observations, adults help them understand that complex situations can be viewed in multiple ways. This supports social learning, empathy, and flexible thinking.

Focus on habits of mind, not memorization.

The purpose of this book is not to have children memorize facts about scenes. The purpose is to help them develop strong habits of mind that support learning in every subject and throughout life.

These habits include:

- looking carefully
- asking thoughtful questions
- noticing relationships
- making predictions
- considering consequences
- thinking ethically
- reflecting before acting

These are life skills as much as academic skills.

A Note About Pace and Progress

Children do not all think in exactly the same way or at the same speed. Some may notice many details quickly. Others may need more time to feel confident sharing their observations. Some may enjoy prediction. Others may be especially interested in emotional or ethical questions.

That is perfectly normal.

This book is not meant to force one type of thinking. It is meant to strengthen thinking in a gradual, supportive, and engaging way.

Adults should feel free to:

- revisit scenes
- continue conversations over multiple days
- connect scenes to real-life experiences

- adapt questions to the age and maturity of the child

The book can be used in classrooms, homeschool settings, tutoring sessions, family discussion time, or individual reflection.

What This Book Is Really Teaching

Although the scenes may appear simple at first, the deeper purpose of the book is much bigger.

This book helps children learn how to:

- observe the world carefully

- think critically about what they see

- understand systems and relationships

- make responsible choices

- Imagine how the future can be shaped by actions today

These are powerful foundations not just for school success, but for life.

When children become strong observers, they also become stronger readers, better problem-solvers, better listeners, and more thoughtful members of their communities.

That is why this book begins with vision, curiosity, and reflection.

Before children learn to read many words, they can begin learning how to read **patterns, systems, relationships, and meaning**.

And that kind of learning can shape the rest of their lives.

The Cognitive Ladder Method

The learning process in this book follows a developmental structure called the **Cognitive Ladder**.

A ladder helps people climb from one level to another step by step. In the same way, the Cognitive Ladder helps the mind gradually develop stronger thinking skills.

Children do not usually begin with advanced reasoning. They begin by noticing. Then, with practice, they learn to interpret, connect, imagine, and understand more deeply.

The Cognitive Ladder organizes that growth into four levels:

1. **Observation**

2. **Inference**

3. **Thematic Synthesis**

4. **Abstract Continuity**

Each level strengthens a different way of thinking and prepares the learner for a more complex understanding.

Rather than asking children to perform difficult reasoning immediately, the Cognitive Ladder builds ability gradually. Students first learn to notice, then to interpret, then to understand deeper meaning, and finally to think creatively and imaginatively about possibilities and consequences.

This step-by-step progression allows learners to build confidence while strengthening important cognitive skills such as attention, reasoning, memory, imagination, and reflection.

By moving through these levels, children learn not only how to see what is in front of them but also how to think about what it might mean and how it might change.

Each scene in this book has been carefully designed to guide learners through these stages.

Level 1: Observation (Scenes 1–5)

At the first level, children practice **careful observation**.

Observation is the foundation of all learning. Before we can understand, explain, or evaluate something, we must first learn to notice it clearly.

Many people look at the world quickly without paying attention to the details. Observation training encourages learners to slow down and look closely.

During this stage, students focus on identifying visible elements in a scene. They learn to notice:

- colors
- shapes
- objects
- people and animals
- position and movement
- size and distance

These exercises help strengthen **attention to detail** and **visual awareness**.

When children practice careful observation, their minds begin to recognize patterns and differences more easily. They become more patient and thoughtful when looking at information. Instead of rushing to judgment, they learn to gather evidence first.

For example, a child might notice that:

- a bird is blue
- A tree is tall
- the sky is clear
- A river is moving gently
- A child is standing near a fence
- The light suggests it is afternoon

At first, these details may seem simple. But they are important because they train the mind to become precise and attentive.

Observation also encourages curiosity. Children begin asking questions such as:

- What else do I see?
- Did I miss anything?
- Where is this happening?
- How are these objects arranged?
- What details seem important?

This level helps children build the mental foundation needed for deeper thinking in the later stages of the Cognitive Ladder.

Without strong observation, later reasoning becomes weak. But when children learn to notice clearly, every higher level becomes stronger.

Level 2: Inference (Scenes 6–10)

At the second level, children begin moving beyond simply noticing what is visible. They start **interpreting clues** and **making predictions**.

This process is called **inference**.

Inference means using evidence from what we see to make reasonable ideas about what might be happening or what might happen next. It is an important thinking skill used in reading, science, history, social situations, and everyday problem-solving.

At this level, learners practice asking questions such as:

- What might happen next?
- Why is something happening?
- What clues suggest a possible outcome?
- What might this person or animal be doing?
- What could change if one part of the scene changes?

For example, if dark clouds gather over a boat, a student may infer that rain is coming and that the people on the boat may need to act quickly.

Inference encourages learners to connect observation with reasoning.

Instead of simply listing what they see, they begin thinking about relationships between events and possible consequences. This develops flexibility in thinking because one situation may lead to several different possible outcomes.

- This level also strengthens:
- problem-solving
- prediction
- evidence-based reasoning
- decision-making

Children begin learning that the world often gives clues, and careful thinkers learn how to notice them.

Level 3: Thematic Synthesis (Scenes 11–15)

At this level, learners move beyond individual details and begin recognizing the **larger meaning, mood, or message** of a scene.

This process is called **thematic synthesis.**

Rather than focusing only on what is visible, students begin asking what the scene communicates.

Some questions they may consider include:

- Does this place feel calm or busy?
- Is this situation safe or dangerous?
- Are the people cooperating or facing a problem?
- What message might the scene communicate?
- What values are present here?

For example, a scene showing children planting trees may suggest themes of:

- teamwork
- care for the environment
- responsibility
- community improvement

A busy marketplace might suggest:

- cooperation

- exchange

- movement

- interdependence

Thematic synthesis strengthens several important skills:

- **Emotional awareness** — recognizing feelings and moods

- **Interpretation** — understanding how details combine to create meaning

- **Comprehension** — seeing connections between actions and larger ideas

- **Ethical reflection** — thinking about what choices and values are present in the scene

At this stage, children begin to understand that events are often part of larger systems and shared human experiences. They also start recognizing that values such as fairness, kindness, cooperation, and responsibility can be visible in scenes and situations.

This deepens both intellectual understanding and social awareness.

Level 4: Abstract Continuity (Scenes 16–20)

The final level of the Cognitive Ladder encourages learners to use **memory, imagination, and creative thinking**.

At this stage, students think beyond the immediate image. Instead of focusing only on what is shown, they begin exploring possibilities, change, and future development.

They may practice:

- recalling scenes from memory

- imagining how the scene could change over time

- visualizing different outcomes

- modifying details in their mind

- predicting future developments

- thinking about consequences across time

For example, students may imagine:

- what a place looks like in another season

- what happens if one key object is removed

- how a community changes after a new building is added

- how people in the scene may solve a problem together

These exercises strengthen:

- mental visualization

- long-term memory

- creative reasoning

- foresight

- planning

More importantly, abstract continuity helps children recognize that the world is always changing. Every situation has a past, a present, and a possible future.

When children imagine different outcomes, they begin to understand that actions today influence what happens tomorrow.

This stage develops some of the most advanced habits of thinking in the book. It encourages learners not only to understand what *is*, but also to consider what *could be*.

Climbing the Cognitive Ladder

The Cognitive Ladder shows how thinking grows step by step.

Each level supports the next:

- Observation teaches children to notice clearly.

- Inference teaches them to reason from clues.

- Thematic Synthesis teaches them to identify deeper meaning.

- Abstract Continuity teaches them to imagine, plan, and think across time.

By practicing these stages regularly, children strengthen skills that are essential for lifelong learning.

They become:

- better observers
- clearer thinkers
- stronger problem-solvers
- more reflective learners
- more thoughtful members of their communities

Learning in this way is not simply about answering questions correctly.

It is about developing the ability to:

- see clearly
- think carefully
- understand systems
- consider consequences
- and act responsibly

The diagram below illustrates the four levels of the Cognitive Ladder, showing how thinking can progress from simple observation to advanced abstract continuity.

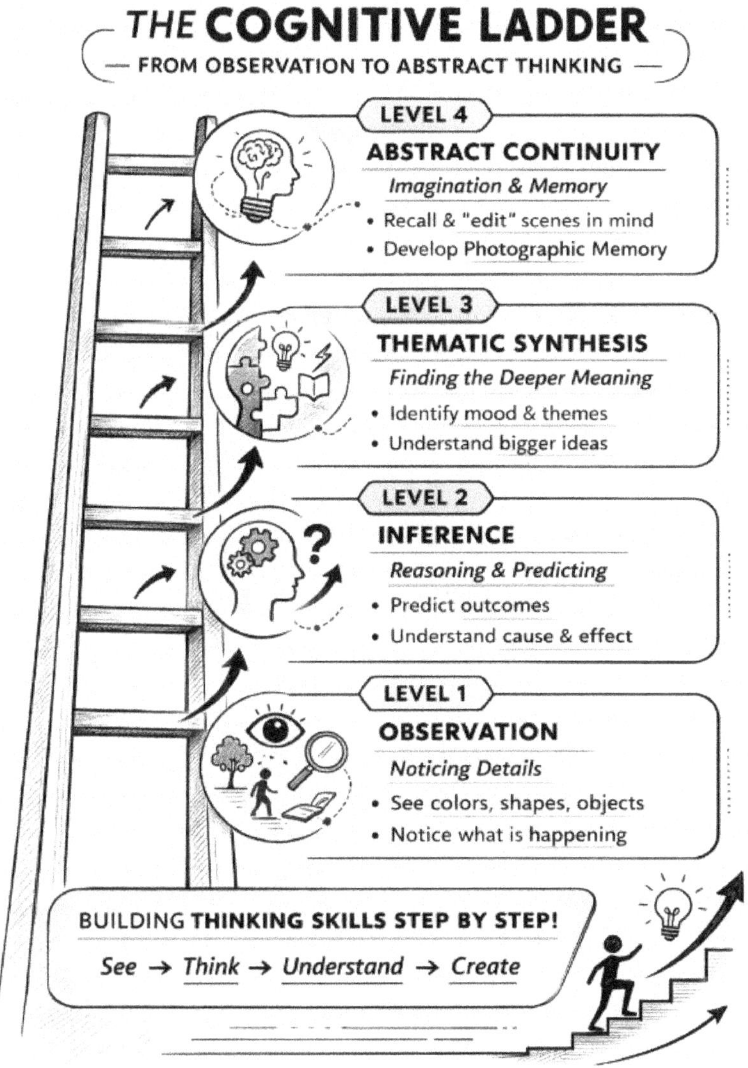

Chapter 1

The Pre-Literacy Visual Audit

From the very beginning of life, human beings learn by watching the world around them. Long before a child can recognize letters or read sentences, their brain is constantly gathering information through sight. Babies observe faces, movements, colors, and shapes. They notice when someone smiles, when objects move, and when something changes in their surroundings.

These early visual experiences are not random. The brain is quietly building connections every moment. A baby slowly learns that a familiar face often means comfort and care. A moving toy attracts attention and curiosity. A bright color may signal something interesting to explore.

As children grow, their minds begin organizing what they see into patterns and relationships. They start recognizing familiar faces and places. They notice repeated actions and routines. Gradually, they begin to understand that certain events often lead to specific outcomes.

For example, they may learn that when clouds gather in the sky, rain sometimes follows. When a door opens, someone may enter the room. When a ball is thrown, it usually falls back to the ground.

This natural learning process forms the early foundation of thinking.

But there is an important difference between **looking** and **observing**.

Looking happens quickly. It is when your eyes scan a scene without much thought. Many people move through the world this way, noticing only what is immediately necessary.

Observing is different.

Observation requires slowing down and paying attention. When you observe, you notice details. You look carefully at how things are arranged. You begin to think about why things are happening and how they might change.

Observation turns simple sight into understanding.

When people observe carefully, they begin to see more than just objects. They start noticing relationships, movement, cause and effect, and patterns that connect different parts of a scene.

And when these patterns begin to appear, something important happens in the mind.

Questions begin to form.

- Why is this happening?
- What caused it?
- What might happen next?
- How are these things connected?

These questions are signs that your brain is actively thinking.

This careful examination of a scene is called a **visual audit.**

A visual audit means studying what you see in order to understand how different parts of a scene interact with each other. Instead of simply noticing objects, you begin thinking about how those objects are connected and how they influence one another.

Strong thinkers often begin by observing details that others overlook. They notice small changes, unusual patterns, or hidden relationships that are not obvious at first glance.

Over time, this skill becomes one of the most powerful tools for understanding the world.

Scientists use observation to understand nature. Engineers observe systems to solve problems. Artists observe light and form to create images. Teachers observe how students learn. Leaders observe how <u>communities</u> function.

In every field of life, careful observation leads to better understanding.

That is why this book begins with visual learning.

Before children learn to read complex words, they can begin learning how to **read patterns, relationships, and systems.**

Seeing the Forest, Not Just the Trees

Imagine standing in the middle of a large forest.

At first glance, you may notice tall trees, green leaves, and animals moving quietly among the branches. You might hear birds singing or the wind rustling through the leaves.

But if you slow down and observe carefully, you begin to notice much more.

Sunlight passes through the leaves and feeds the plants growing below.

Plants provide food for insects and animals.

Animals move through the forest spreading seeds that grow into new plants and trees.

Rivers and streams carry water that nourishes plants, animals, and soil.

Suddenly the forest no longer appears to be a random collection of living things.

Instead, it becomes a **system** where every part plays a role.

Each element supports another.

Plants depend on sunlight and water.

Animals depend on plants or other animals for food.

Trees help maintain the soil and provide shelter for countless creatures.

Even fallen leaves contribute to the system. Over time they break down and return nutrients to the soil, helping new plants grow.

When we begin seeing these relationships, the forest becomes more than just a beautiful place.

It becomes a **living network** where many parts work together.

This understanding also reveals something important: small changes in one part of the system can affect many other parts.

If too many trees are removed, animals may lose their homes.

If water becomes scarce, plants may struggle to grow.

If pollution enters a stream, it may harm fish, birds, and animals that depend on clean water.

By observing these connections, we begin to understand how delicate and interconnected natural systems can be.

And the same type of thinking that helps us understand a forest can also help us understand cities, communities, technology, and human behavior.

Observing in Everyday Life

A visual audit is not something that only scientists or researchers perform.

Anyone can practice it.

In fact, the best place to begin practicing observation is in everyday life.

At home, you might watch how your pet interacts with its toys or with people in the room. You may notice that certain sounds attract its attention, or that it prefers certain places to rest.

At school, you might observe how your classmates move, talk, or work together during lessons or group activities. You may begin noticing patterns in how people communicate, cooperate, or solve problems.

In your neighborhood, you might watch cars, bicycles, and pedestrians moving through the streets. Traffic lights guide vehicles to stop and go. Pedestrians wait for signals before crossing. Drivers adjust their speed to avoid collisions.

These everyday scenes contain countless small interactions that keep systems running smoothly.

Even simple activities can train your brain to notice details and relationships.

Over time, these observations help you develop another important skill: **prediction.**

When you notice patterns in events, you begin to predict what might happen next.

For example:

If a ball begins rolling down a hill, you can predict that it will continue moving until something stops it.

If dark clouds gather and the wind becomes strong, you may predict that rain or a storm could follow.

Prediction helps people make decisions and avoid problems. It is one of the foundations of critical thinking.

Exercises to Build Your Observation Skills

Observation improves with practice.

Just like muscles grow stronger with exercise, the brain becomes better at noticing details when we train it regularly.

The following activities are simple ways to strengthen your observation skills.

The "Five Things" Game

Look around a room, a park, or a classroom.

List five things you notice that you have never noticed before.

These could be small details such as:

- the pattern on a wall
- the shape of leaves on a tree
- the way sunlight reflects on a window
- the sound of wind moving through branches
- the way shadows fall across the ground

After listing these details, ask yourself:

How might these objects be connected?

Even small details may be part of larger systems.

Predict the Outcome

Watch a small event carefully.

It could be water flowing through a stream, leaves falling from a tree, or a ball rolling down a slope.

Before the event finishes, try to predict what will happen next.

Then observe whether your prediction was correct.

This exercise trains the brain to connect **observation with reasoning.**

Connect the Dots

Draw a simple scene you see around you, such as your classroom, your backyard, or a playground.

After drawing the objects in the scene, draw arrows or lines showing how different parts interact.

For example:

- Trees provide shade for people sitting nearby.
- Birds rest on branches and eat insects.
- People walk along paths to avoid damaging the grass.
- Water fountains provide drinking water for visitors.

This activity helps your brain recognize systems and relationships.

Preparing for the Scenes Ahead

In this book, we will explore twenty scenes that take place in different environments.

Some will show natural landscapes. Others will show human communities and busy places where many things happen at once.

Each scene is designed to help you practice important thinking skills.

You will learn to:

- observe carefully

- notice details others might miss

- understand how different parts connect

- predict what might happen next

These skills will help you move beyond simply seeing the world.

They will help you begin **reading the world.**

Just as reading words helps you understand stories, observing carefully helps you understand how real-life systems work.

When you begin recognizing relationships between objects, people, and events, your understanding becomes deeper and more meaningful.

Let us begin exploring the first scenes that will train your observation skills.

Scenes 1–5: Observation

Focus: Identifying visible details

During these first scenes, your goal is simple: notice as many details as possible.

Try to identify objects, animals, people, and environmental features before thinking about deeper meanings.

Careful observation is the first step toward understanding complex systems.

Scene 1: The Forest Clearing

Imagine standing in a quiet forest clearing.

Tall oak and pine trees surround you, their branches stretching high into the sky. Leaves flutter gently in the breeze, creating soft rustling sounds. Sunlight filters through small openings in the canopy above, forming shifting patterns of light and shadow on the forest floor.

Birds hop between branches, searching for insects. Squirrels scamper along tree trunks and leap from branch to branch. Tiny insects crawl across fallen leaves, quietly performing their role in the forest ecosystem.

A rabbit cautiously peeks from behind a bush, its ears alert for danger. Nearby, a small stream bubbles gently as it flows between stones, providing water for animals and nourishing nearby plants.

The forest may appear peaceful, but many small interactions are taking place at once.

Observation Exercise

List **10 details** you can identify:

Examples may include:

- trees
- birds
- insects
- sunlight patterns
- fallen leaves
- the rabbit
- the stream
- rocks near the water
- bushes and plants
- shadows on the ground

Identify 3 relationships

Examples:

Sunlight —> plants grow

Plants —> insects feed

Stream —> animals drink water

Reflection Questions

1. How does sunlight influence the plants and animals in this scene?
2. What connections can you see between the forest creatures?
3. Which small details might be easy to miss at first glance?

Scene 2: The Playground

Picture a lively school playground on a bright sunny day.

Children swing high on playground swings while others climb jungle gyms and ladders. A group of students plays hopscotch, carefully jumping from square to square. Nearby, another group runs across the field chasing a bright red ball.

Teachers stand nearby, watching carefully to ensure that everyone stays safe. Laughter fills the air as children explore, run, and play together.

Near the fence, a small dog wanders curiously, sniffing the ground. Trees surrounding the playground provide patches of shade where children pause to rest.

A bird perches quietly on the top of an empty swing, watching the activity below.

Observation Exercise

List **10 details** you see.

Examples:

- swings
- jungle gym
- children playing
- teachers watching
- a ball
- a dog
- trees
- shade
- hopscotch squares
- bird on a swing

Identify 3 relationships

Examples:

Children —> swings —> movement

Teachers —> children —> safety

Trees —> shade —> resting

Reflection Questions

1. How do the children's actions affect others around them?

2. What patterns do you notice in the movement of children and animals?

3. How do adults help maintain safety and order?

Scene 3: The Busy Street

Imagine standing on a bustling city street.

Cars move steadily through traffic while bicycles weave carefully between lanes. Pedestrians walk quickly along sidewalks, heading to shops, offices, or homes.

Street vendors call out to passersby, offering fruits, toys, books, and snacks. The sounds of conversation, footsteps, and engines blend into the busy rhythm of city life.

Pigeons gather near the sidewalk, pecking at crumbs left behind by visitors. Trees planted along the street provide shade for pedestrians and help cool the air.

In the distance, a construction site hums with activity as workers build new structures.

Observation Exercise

List **10 details** you see.

Examples:

- cars
- bicycles
- pedestrians
- vendors
- pigeons
- trees
- construction workers

- shops
- sidewalks
- traffic signs

Identify 3 relationships

Cars —> traffic flow —> safety

Vendors —> customers —> income

Trees —> shade —> comfort

Reflection Questions

1. How do humans and animals share this space?
2. What patterns of movement can you identify?
3. How might one small change affect the entire street?

Scene 4: The Farm

Visualize a peaceful farm at sunrise.

Golden sunlight spreads across open fields where cows graze quietly. Chickens wander through the yard, pecking at the ground in search of food.

The farmer waters crops while a tractor moves slowly between rows of growing plants. A nearby stream provides water that nourishes both animals and crops.

Birds glide through the sky above the fields. A dog runs across the yard, playfully chasing a rabbit that darts into the tall grass.

Trees lining the property mark natural boundaries and provide shade.

Observation Exercise

List **10 details** you notice.

Examples:

- cows
- chickens
- farmer

- tractor
- crops
- stream
- dog
- rabbit
- birds
- trees

Identify 3 relationships

Stream —> crops —> growth

Crops —> animals —> food

Dog —> rabbit —> chase

Reflection Questions

1. How does each part of the farm depend on the others?
2. What cycles can you see between animals and plants?
3. Which small interactions help the farm run smoothly?

Scene 5: The Neighborhood Park

Picture a neighborhood park in the late afternoon.

Children ride bicycles along winding paths while parents spread blankets on the grass for picnics. The sound of laughter mixes with the gentle splash of a fountain in the center of the park.

Squirrels dart between tree branches searching for food. Birds sing overhead while ducks glide across the pond.

Joggers move steadily along walking paths, and groups of friends throw frisbees across open fields.

People feed ducks near the water's edge while others sit quietly enjoying the peaceful surroundings.

Observation Exercise

List **10 details** you see.

- Examples:
- bicycles
- picnic blankets
- fountain
- squirrels
- birds
- ducks
- joggers
- walking paths
- frisbees
- pond

Identify 3 relationships

Fountain —> water —> birds

Paths —> joggers —> safety

Trees —> squirrels —> shelter

Reflection Questions

1. How do people and animals share this space?
2. What patterns of activity do you notice?
3. Which actions depend on one another to happen safely?

CHAPTER 2

Developing the Photographic Anchor

Your brain has an extraordinary ability: it can store images in memory in a way that allows you to recall not just a single detail, but an entire scene.

Think of this ability as your mind's own camera. When you look at something carefully, your brain can capture the shapes, colors, positions, and relationships between objects. Later, you can return to that image in your mind and explore it again, almost as if you were still looking at it.

These powerful mental images are called **photographic anchors**.

A photographic anchor is more than a simple memory. It is a mental snapshot that contains many layers of information at once. It includes not only what things look like, but also how they interact, what emotions might be present, and how the environment around them behaves.

Unlike fleeting memories that disappear quickly, a strong photographic anchor allows the mind to return to the same image repeatedly and examine it from different perspectives.

For example, imagine that you observe a park scene carefully. You notice children playing, trees swaying in the wind, birds flying overhead, and people walking along a path.

Later, if that scene has become a photographic anchor in your mind, you may be able to recall:

- where the children were standing

- which direction the wind was blowing

- how the trees were arranged

- where the birds were flying

- how people moved through the space

Your brain can revisit the scene and continue thinking about it even when the image itself is no longer in front of you.

This ability to hold an image in your mind and explore it thoroughly is one of the most powerful cognitive tools a person can develop.

Why Photographic Anchors Matter

Children who learn to build strong photographic anchors develop more than memory.

They develop the ability to:

- understand complex situations

- notice relationships between events

- anticipate possible outcomes

- reflect on cause and effect

- imagine different possibilities for the future

These skills are useful not only in school subjects such as science, reading, and history, but also in everyday decision-making.

For example, when children observe situations carefully, they begin to recognize patterns. They may notice that certain behaviors lead to certain results. They may remember how problems were solved before and apply those ideas in new situations.

Photographic anchors make thinking more flexible and powerful because they allow the brain to work with **complete scenes rather than isolated pieces of information**.

Instead of remembering only a single detail, the brain remembers how everything in the scene fits together.

Building Strong Anchors Through Attention

Strong photographic anchors do not happen by accident. They develop when we give our full attention to what we see.

Attention is like a spotlight in the mind. When we focus carefully on a scene, the brain records more information. Colors appear sharper. Movements become clearer. Relationships between objects become easier to notice.

When attention is weak, memory becomes weak as well. The mind may glance quickly at something without really understanding it.

But when we slow down and observe carefully, the brain gathers richer information.

This is why the earlier exercises in observation were so important. They trained the mind to notice details that might otherwise be ignored.

Observation strengthens the first step of the Cognitive Ladder. Photographic anchors strengthen the next step by helping the brain **store and revisit what it observed**.

The Cognitive Ladder in Action

The Cognitive Ladder helps children move from simple observation to deeper thinking.

Let us briefly revisit the four levels and see how photographic anchors support them.

Observation

First, we observe the scene carefully. We identify objects, colors, movements, and positions.

This stage creates the initial visual information.

Inference

Next, we begin asking questions about what might be happening.

We think about cause and effect. We imagine what might happen next.

Photographic anchors allow us to hold the entire scene in mind while we make these predictions.

Thematic Understanding

After noticing details and predicting outcomes, we begin to understand the deeper meaning or theme of the scene.

We may recognize cooperation, danger, calmness, teamwork, or responsibility.

Abstract Thinking

Finally, we imagine how the situation could change over time.

We think about possible futures and the consequences of different actions.

Photographic anchors make this process easier because the mind can return to the original scene and mentally adjust it in different ways.

Strengthening Memory Through Visualization

Visualization is the ability to picture something in your mind.

When children practice visualizing scenes, they strengthen the brain's ability to store and recall information. Visualization also helps children explore ideas creatively.

For example, after observing a garden scene, a child might imagine:

- what the garden looks like in the evening
- how it changes during a rainstorm
- how animals behave when the weather changes
- how plants grow over time

By mentally revisiting and adjusting the scene, children practice both memory and imagination.

This process strengthens the brain's ability to connect observation with reasoning.

From Observation to Inference

In the next set of scenes, you will begin practicing **inference**.

Inference means using clues to predict what might happen next.

When you observe carefully and remember the scene clearly, you can begin asking questions such as:

- What might happen if something changes?
- How might the people or animals respond?
- What events could follow this situation?

Inference connects observation with reasoning.

Instead of simply describing what you see, you begin thinking about how events may unfold.

This skill is important not only for learning but also for everyday decision-making. Many wise decisions are based on the ability to anticipate consequences before they occur.

Let us now explore several new scenes and practice making thoughtful predictions.

Scenes 6–10: Inference

Focus: Predicting outcomes and consequences

In these scenes, you will still begin by observing details.

But now you will take the next step: imagining what might happen next.

Think carefully about the clues you see in each scene. Small details may suggest important possibilities.

Scene 6: The Garden

Imagine a small backyard garden.

Rows of flowers bloom in bright colors. Bees buzz from flower to flower, collecting nectar. Butterflies rest gently on petals before floating into the air again.

Near the garden, a small pond reflects sunlight. Frogs sit on smooth stones at the water's edge while dragonflies glide above the surface.

A cat naps peacefully under a bush, its tail occasionally twitching in the warm sunlight. Nearby, a watering can rests beside a patch of newly planted vegetables.

Leaves rustle gently as a light breeze moves through the garden.

Observation Exercise

List **10 details** you notice:

Examples may include:

- flowers
- bees
- butterflies
- pond
- frogs
- dragonflies
- cat under the bush
- watering can
- vegetables
- sunlight

Identify 3 relationships

Flowers —> bees —> pollination

Pond —> frogs —> insects

Cat —> shade —> resting

Inference Challenge

Now imagine a change.

What might happen if dark clouds suddenly appear and rain begins?

Consider these questions:

- How might the bees and butterflies respond to rain?
- What might happen to the cat resting under the bush?
- How might the plants benefit from the rainfall?

Thinking about these possibilities helps you connect observation with prediction.

Scene 7: The River Crossing

A clear river winds through a dense forest.

Fish swim beneath the surface while deer approach the water's edge to drink. Birds glide overhead searching for insects.

A wooden bridge stretches across the river, allowing people to cross safely. On the riverbank, fallen logs create small paths that animals use to move between trees.

The forest is calm, but the flowing water reminds us that nature is always changing.

Observation Exercise

List **10 details** you see.

Examples:

- river
- fish
- deer
- birds
- bridge
- trees
- logs
- water movement
- plants
- rocks

Identify 3 relationships

River —> plants —> animals

Bridge —> humans —> safe crossing

Logs —> animals —> pathways

Inference Challenge

Imagine heavy rain begins in the mountains upstream.

Ask yourself:

- How might rising water levels affect the river?
- What could happen to the bridge?
- How might animals change their paths?

Thinking about these changes helps you understand how natural systems respond to environmental conditions.

Scene 8: The Busy Market

A lively marketplace fills a town square.

Stalls display colorful fruits, vegetables, clothes, and toys. Vendors call out to customers while people move through the crowd carrying baskets and bags.

A street musician plays cheerful music nearby, attracting listeners who pause to enjoy the sound. The scent of fresh bread drifts through the air from a bakery stall.

Dogs wander between booths, hoping to find dropped food. Children weave through the crowd, chasing one another.

The market is full of movement, conversation, and activity.

Observation Exercise

List **12 details** in the scene.

- Examples:
- fruit stalls
- vegetables
- vendors
- shoppers
- baskets
- street musician
- dogs

- children
- bakery
- bread
- music
- crowd

Identify 3 connections

Buyers —> sellers —> trade

Musician —> shoppers —> lively mood

Food stalls —> customers —> activity

Inference Challenge

Imagine a sudden rainstorm begins.

Ask yourself:

- How might vendors protect their goods?
- Where might people move to find shelter?
- Which stalls might be affected first?

Thinking through these possibilities helps you understand how people adapt to changing conditions.

Scene 9: The Construction Site

A construction site hums with activity.

Large machines dig trenches while cranes lift heavy materials into place. Workers wearing helmets and bright safety vests coordinate their tasks carefully.

Dust rises from the ground as trucks move back and forth carrying supplies.

Nearby, a fence separates the construction area from a sidewalk where curious children watch the machines from a safe distance.

Trees sway gently in the breeze around the site.

Observation Exercise

List **10 details**.

Examples:

- cranes
- trucks
- workers
- helmets
- safety vests
- trenches
- fence
- children watching
- trees
- dust

Identify 3 relationships

Machines —> work speed —> progress

Workers —> machines —> safety

Fence —> children —> protection

Inference Challenge

Imagine one machine is left unattended while still running.
Ask yourself:

- What problems could occur?
- How might this affect workers or equipment?
- What safety rules might prevent accidents?

Thinking about these questions helps build responsible awareness

Scene 10: The School Playground

Children laugh and play on a busy school playground.

Some swing high into the air while others climb ladders and slide down brightly colored slides. A soccer ball rolls across the grass as a group of children chase after it.

Teachers stand nearby watching the activity and guiding students when necessary.

Birds perch in nearby trees while leaves rustle in the wind. A curious cat sits quietly on the fence, observing the movement below.

Every action on the playground affects another.

Observation Exercise

List **10 details**.

Examples:

- swings
- slides
- ladders
- soccer ball
- children
- teachers
- trees
- birds
- cat
- grass

Identify 3 relationships

Children —> swings —> movement

Teachers —> supervision —> safety

Ball —> players —> activity

Inference Challenge

Now imagine dark clouds gather and rain begins suddenly.

Ask yourself:

- How will the children react?
- What might teachers do to keep everyone safe?
- Which parts of the playground could become slippery?

Thinking ahead like this helps train the mind to anticipate outcomes and make responsible choices.

Scenes 11–15: Thematic Synthesis

Focus: Recognizing meaning, mood, and patterns

In the previous scenes, you practiced observing details and predicting what might happen next. These skills are important steps in learning how to think carefully.

Now you will move to the next level of the Cognitive Ladder: **Thematic Synthesis**.

At this level, you begin to look at an entire scene and ask a different type of question.

Instead of focusing only on individual objects, you begin asking:

- What is the overall feeling of this place?
- What story might this scene be telling?
- What message might it communicate?
- What patterns connect the people, animals, and environment?

Thematic synthesis means combining many small observations into a larger understanding.

Think of it as stepping back from a puzzle after placing many pieces together. Suddenly, you see the full picture.

Scenes at this level encourage children to notice emotions, patterns of cooperation, challenges, and relationships within environments. These reflections help build emotional awareness and ethical thinking.

Let us explore the next scenes.

Scene 11: The Sunset Beach

Imagine standing on a quiet beach as the sun begins to set.

The sky glows with shades of orange, pink, and gold. Gentle waves roll toward the shore, leaving delicate patterns in the sand. Seagulls circle overhead, their wings catching the warm light of the evening.

Children kneel near the water, carefully building sandcastles. Parents sit nearby on blankets, reading or watching the horizon. In the distance, a lighthouse sends a steady beam of light across the ocean.

The air feels calm and peaceful. The sounds of the waves and distant birds create a quiet rhythm.

Observation Exercise

List **10 details** you notice.

Examples may include:

- sunset colors
- waves
- sandcastles
- children
- parents
- lighthouse
- seagulls
- blankets
- ocean horizon
- footprints in sand

Identify 3 relationships

Examples:

Waves —> sand —> sandcastle building

Sunlight —> ocean —> reflections

Parents —> children —> supervision

Thematic Challenge

Now step back and consider the entire scene.

Ask yourself:

- What mood does this place create?

- Does the environment feel calm, joyful, or peaceful?

- How do the colors and sounds affect how people behave?

- What lesson might this scene suggest about enjoying nature and spending time together?

This type of reflection helps us understand how environments influence emotions and experiences.

Scene 12: The Rainy Street

Imagine a city street during a gentle rain.

People walk along the sidewalks holding umbrellas of many colors. Cars move slowly through puddles, sending small splashes of water toward the curb.

Streetlights reflect on the wet pavement, creating shimmering patterns across the road.

A bus stops near the corner as passengers hurry to board. Nearby, two children laugh as they jump into puddles, sending water splashing into the air.

Even though the rain changes the environment, life in the city continues.

Observation Exercise

List **10 details**.

Examples:

- umbrellas

- rain

- puddles

- cars

- streetlights

- bus
- sidewalks
- reflections
- children splashing
- buildings

Identify 3 relationships

Rain —> puddles —> children playing

Streetlights —> water —> reflections

Bus —> passengers —> transportation

Thematic Challenge

Consider the overall scene.

Ask yourself:

- What mood does this environment create?
- How does rain change people's behavior?
- Do people move faster, slower, or differently?
- What lesson might this scene suggest about adapting to unexpected situations?

This stage encourages learners to recognize how conditions influence human behavior.

Scene 13: The Library

Imagine entering a quiet library.

Tall shelves filled with books stretch from floor to ceiling. Students sit at wooden tables reading or writing in notebooks. The room is calm and focused.

A librarian helps a child search for a book while sunlight streams gently through large windows.

A clock ticks softly on the wall, marking the passage of time.

The atmosphere feels peaceful, thoughtful, and full of possibility.

Observation Exercise

List **10 details**.

- Examples:
- bookshelves
- students reading
- tables
- notebooks
- librarian
- windows
- sunlight
- clock
- chairs
- quiet environment

Identify 3 relationships

Students —> books —> learning

Librarian —> child —> guidance

Sunlight —> environment —> calm mood

Thematic Challenge

Think about the meaning of this scene.

Ask yourself:

- What feeling does this place create?
- How does a quiet environment support learning?
- What message might this scene communicate about curiosity and knowledge?

Scenes like this help children understand how environments can encourage focus and discovery.

Scene 14: The Festival

Imagine a colorful community festival.

Bright banners hang across the streets while music fills the air. Food stalls release delicious smells of fresh bread, roasted corn, and sweet desserts.

Children run through the crowd chasing balloons while families laugh and talk together.

A performer dressed as a clown entertains a group of young children, making them laugh with silly tricks.

People dance, sing, and celebrate together.

The entire space feels energetic and joyful.

Observation Exercise

List **10 details**.

Examples:

- banners
- music
- food stalls
- balloons
- children
- families
- clown performer
- dancing
- crowds
- colorful decorations

Identify 3 relationships

Music —> dancing —> celebration

Food —> people —> gathering

Performers —> audience —> entertainment

Thematic Challenge

Consider the bigger meaning of this scene.

Ask yourself:

- What mood does this event create?

- How do shared celebrations bring communities together?

- What does this scene show about cooperation and happiness?

Festivals often reflect the values and traditions of communities.

Scene 15: The Mountain Hike

Imagine a winding trail climbing through a mountain landscape.

Hikers carry backpacks as they follow a narrow path upward. Wildflowers grow beside the trail while birds circle high above the peaks.

Nearby, a waterfall cascades down a rocky cliff, creating a cool mist that drifts through the air.

Clouds move slowly across the sky as sunlight breaks through in soft beams.

The environment feels vast, quiet, and inspiring.

Observation Exercise

List **10 details**.

Examples:

- trail

- hikers

- backpacks

- waterfall

- birds

- clouds

- wildflowers

- mountains

- rocks
- sunlight

Identify 3 relationships

Waterfall —> water —> plants

Trail —> hikers —> movement

Mountains —> environment —> exploration

Thematic Challenge

Ask yourself:

- What feeling does this landscape create?
- Does it suggest adventure, calmness, or determination?
- What lesson might this scene teach about perseverance and exploration?

Nature often encourages reflection and resilience.

Scenes 16–20: Abstract Continuity

Focus: Memory, imagination, and future thinking

The final stage of the Cognitive Ladder is **Abstract Continuity**.

At this level, learners move beyond observation, prediction, and thematic understanding. They begin using imagination and memory to explore how scenes could change over time.

Abstract continuity encourages children to:

recall scenes from memory

imagine different possibilities

mentally adjust details

think about future outcomes

These exercises strengthen mental visualization and creative reasoning.

Let us explore the final scenes.

Scene 16: The Night Sky

Picture a clear night sky above a grassy hill.

Stars sparkle across the dark sky like scattered diamonds. A crescent moon glows softly above the horizon.

A child stands beside a telescope pointing toward a constellation.

Suddenly, a shooting star streaks across the sky before fading into darkness.

Leaves rustle quietly in the night breeze.

Memory Exercise

Close your eyes and try to recall the scene.

Imagine:

- the position of the moon
- the telescope
- the child
- the stars
- the shooting star

Now imagine a change.

What if the shooting star appeared in a different part of the sky?

How would that change the child's reaction?

This exercise strengthens memory and visualization.

Scene 17: The City at Night

Imagine a tall city skyline glowing in the darkness.

Lights shine from windows high above the streets. Cars move through the city like streams of light as their headlights reflect off the pavement.

A river flows quietly beside the city while a large bridge arches across the water.

The lights of buildings reflect in the river's surface.

Memory Exercise

Visualize the scene again in your mind.

Ask yourself:

- Where are the brightest lights?
- Where are the cars moving?
- How does the bridge connect the two sides of the river?

Now imagine a change.

What if a boat appeared on the river?

How would its lights reflect in the water?

Scene 18: The Desert Oasis

Picture an enormous desert filled with golden sand dunes.

In the center of the desert lies a small oasis. A pool of clear water sits beneath several tall palm trees.

Animals gather near the water to drink. The hot air shimmers above the sand.

The oasis creates a rare and valuable place of life in the middle of a dry landscape.

Memory Exercise

Try recalling the scene clearly.

Imagine:

- the dunes
- the palm trees
- the water
- the animals

Now imagine a traveler approaching the oasis.

How might the animals react?

How would the traveler benefit from finding water in the desert?

Scene 19: The Snowy Village

Visualize a small village covered in fresh snow.

Smoke rises from the chimneys of cozy cottages. Children laugh as they roll snowballs and build snowmen.

Animals leave tracks across the snowy ground while warm lights glow from cottage windows.

Snow continues to fall slowly from the sky.

Memory Exercise

Recall the scene carefully.

Now imagine a stronger snowstorm arriving.

How might villagers prepare?

Where might animals find shelter?

How might the village change the next morning?

Scene 20: The Space Station

Imagine a space station floating high above Earth.

Astronauts drift weightlessly inside the station as they work with computers and scientific equipment.

Outside the station, satellites orbit slowly while the blue curve of Earth rotates below.

The atmosphere glows softly where sunlight meets the edge of the planet.

Memory Exercise

Visualize the scene clearly.

Now imagine changes:

- What if a satellite moves closer to the station?
- What tasks might astronauts perform?
- How does the station depend on careful coordination?

This final scene encourages children to imagine systems operating far beyond everyday environments.

CHAPTER 3

Understanding Systems and Ethics

Everything around us is connected in ways that are sometimes easy to see and sometimes hidden beneath the surface. Trees, animals, rivers, roads, schools, homes, and people all form systems—groups of parts that work together to achieve a purpose.

When you begin to understand systems, you start to see the world differently. Instead of viewing things as separate pieces, you begin to notice how they interact and influence one another. You see networks of relationships rather than isolated events.

At first, many parts of life may seem unrelated.

A tree stands quietly in one place.

A bird flies overhead.

A car drives down a road.

A student walks into a classroom.

Each of these actions might appear separate at first glance. But when we observe more carefully, we begin to see that they are connected through larger systems.

The tree provides shelter and food for birds and insects.

Insects help pollinate plants.

Plants support animals and humans by producing oxygen and food.

Roads allow people to travel to work, school, and markets.

Schools help communities grow by providing knowledge and skills.

When we begin noticing these connections, our understanding of the world becomes deeper and more meaningful. Instead of seeing isolated events, we begin recognizing patterns of interaction that shape how systems function.

This awareness helps us realize that our actions also influence the systems we are part of.

What Is a System?

A **system** is a group of parts that interact with one another to form a working whole.

Systems exist everywhere in the world around us.

Nature is full of systems. Forest ecosystems connect plants, animals, water, soil, and sunlight. Each element contributes to the health and balance of the environment.

Cities contain systems that guide transportation, communication, and trade. Traffic lights, roads, buses, bicycles, and pedestrians all interact to help people move safely through the city.

Schools function as systems that support learning, cooperation, and growth. Teachers, students, books, schedules, and classrooms all contribute to the educational environment.

Even families form systems. Each member contributes in different ways to the well-being of the group through cooperation, support, and communication.

In every system, each part plays a role. When these parts work together effectively, the system functions smoothly.

To understand how systems operate, it helps to look at simple examples.

Imagine a small garden.

The garden includes plants, insects, soil, water, sunlight, and animals.

Sunlight helps plants grow by providing energy for photosynthesis.

Plants produce nectar that feeds insects.

Insects help pollinate flowers so plants can reproduce.

Water nourishes plant roots and supports growth.

Soil provides nutrients that help plants stay healthy.

Each part contributes to the success of the entire system.

If one part changes, other parts respond.

If there is not enough water, plants may struggle to grow.

If insects disappear, pollination may slow down.

If plants become unhealthy, animals may lose important food sources.

This example shows how systems depend on balance. When one part changes, the effects often spread to other parts.

Understanding systems helps us recognize that even small changes can influence many parts of the environment.

The Ripple Effect

One important feature of systems is something called the **ripple effect**.

A ripple effect occurs when one small change spreads outward and influences many other parts of a system.

Imagine dropping a stone into a calm pond. Small waves spread outward in circles across the water.

In systems, actions can create similar effects.

A new road may change how people travel through a city. Businesses may develop nearby, traffic patterns may shift, and neighborhoods may grow.

A new rule in a classroom may change how students behave. If students are encouraged to collaborate, teamwork may improve, and learning may become more enjoyable.

A drought may affect plants, animals, and people who depend on water. Crops may struggle to grow, animals may move to new areas, and communities may need to find alternative water sources.

Even small positive actions can create ripple effects.

Cleaning a park may encourage others to keep the area clean. Visitors may enjoy the space more, animals may live in a healthier environment, and the community may feel greater pride in the shared space.

These examples show that small decisions can have wide consequences.

This understanding encourages people to think carefully before acting.

When we recognize how systems work, we begin asking more thoughtful questions:

- What might happen if this part changes?
- Who might be affected by this decision?
- Could this action create problems somewhere else?
- Could this action improve the system for others?

These questions help develop responsible thinking and encourage us to consider the broader effects of our actions.

Introducing Ethics

Understanding systems naturally leads us to another important idea: **ethics**.

Ethics is the practice of making thoughtful choices that consider how actions affect others and the world around us.

Ethical thinking encourages people to pause before acting and ask questions about responsibility and fairness.

For example:

- Is this choice fair to everyone involved?
- Could this action harm someone else?
- How might this decision affect the environment?
- What might happen if many people made the same choice?

These questions help us think beyond our own immediate needs and consider the well-being of others.

Ethical thinking also encourages empathy. When we imagine how our actions affect other people, animals, or environments, we become more aware of our responsibilities within a system.

Ethics does not always provide simple answers. Many real-world situations require careful thought, discussion, and reflection.

Sometimes different choices may each have advantages and disadvantages. In these situations, ethical thinking helps people evaluate possible outcomes and choose the option that supports fairness, responsibility, and long-term well-being.

By practicing ethical reasoning, individuals develop the habit of making decisions that contribute positively to their communities and environments.

Systems Thinking and Ethical Thinking

Systems thinking and ethical thinking work best when they are combined.

Systems thinking helps us understand **how things work together**.

Ethical thinking helps us decide **how we should act within those systems**.

Together, these two ways of thinking guide responsible decision-making.

For example, imagine someone throwing trash into a river.

Systems thinking helps us understand what could happen next.

The trash may pollute the water.

Fish and plants may be harmed.

Animals that drink the water may become sick.

People who rely on the river may lose a clean source of water.

Ethical thinking helps guide our response.

If we care about the health of the environment and the people who depend on it, we choose not to pollute the river. Instead, we dispose of waste responsibly and help protect natural resources.

By combining systems thinking with ethical reflection, we become better able to make decisions that protect both human communities and natural environments.

Exploring Systems Through Observation

In this chapter, you will examine scenes that show how people, animals, objects, and environments interact within systems.

Some scenes represent **natural systems**, such as forests, rivers, and ecosystems.

Other scenes represent **human systems**, such as transportation networks, schools, markets, and communities.

By studying these scenes carefully, you will practice several important skills:

- identifying connections between parts of a system
- thinking about cause and effect
- predicting how changes might affect the system
- reflecting on ethical responsibilities

These activities build directly on the skills developed earlier in the Cognitive Ladder.

Observation allows you to notice details and relationships.

Inference helps you predict possible outcomes.

Thematic understanding helps you recognize patterns and meaning within situations.

Abstract thinking helps you imagine how systems change over time and how actions today may influence the future.

Together, these skills help you understand complex situations and make thoughtful decisions.

Legacy Learning: Thinking Beyond the Present

Learning about systems and ethics also introduces an important concept called **Legacy Learning**.

Legacy Learning means understanding that our actions today can influence the future.

Every generation inherits a world shaped by the choices of those who came before them.

Cities were built by earlier generations.

Forests were protected—or damaged—by decisions made in the past.

Technologies were developed by people who imagined new possibilities.

The same will be true for the future.

The choices people make today will influence the world that future generations experience.

When children develop habits of systems thinking and ethical reflection, they become more capable of making decisions that protect communities, preserve natural resources, and encourage cooperation.

Legacy Learning encourages us to ask an important question:

What kind of world do we want to help create?

By practicing thoughtful observation and ethical reasoning, individuals can contribute to systems that support healthier environments, stronger communities, and more responsible decision-making.

From Understanding to Action

Understanding ideas is only the beginning.

Real learning happens when knowledge is put into practice.

The exercises in this chapter are designed to help you apply systems thinking and ethical reasoning to real situations.

Each activity invites you to observe a situation carefully, think about cause and effect, and consider the ethical choices available.

As you work through these exercises, remember the thinking process you have been practicing:

- Observe the details carefully.
- Identify relationships between parts of the system.
- Think about cause and effect.
- Reflect on ethical responsibilities.

There is not always one perfect answer.

The goal is to strengthen your ability to think deeply and consider how actions influence the larger system.

Practice Exercises: Systems and Ethical Thinking

Exercise 1 – The Community Park

A community park has only a few trash bins. On busy days, visitors sometimes leave litter on the ground.

Consider the situation carefully.

Questions to think about:

- Where might a new trash bin help reduce litter the most?
- How might this improve the park environment?
- How would cleaner spaces benefit animals and visitors?

This exercise encourages thinking about how small improvements can strengthen an entire system.

Exercise 2 – The School Clubs

Two popular school clubs meet at the same time each week.

Some students want to participate in both clubs but cannot attend both meetings.

Questions to consider:

- How might this schedule affect students?
- What changes could make participation more fair?
- How can school systems be adjusted to benefit more people?

This exercise encourages thinking about fairness and cooperation.

Exercise 3 – Protecting the River

A local river runs through a town where factories operate nearby. Some waste from the factories begins entering the water.

Questions to consider:

- How might pollution affect fish, plants, and animals?
- How could it affect people who rely on the river?
- What solutions might balance industry needs with environmental protection?

This exercise encourages students to think about environmental responsibility and long-term consequences.

The Cognitive Ladder and Ethical Thinking

The thinking skills developed earlier in the book continue to guide learning in this chapter.

The Cognitive Ladder helps connect visual understanding with responsible action.

Level	Thinking Focus	Example
Observation	Identify details	Notice trees, people, and trash in a park
Inference	Predict outcomes	Trash may attract animals or create pollution
Thematic Understanding	Recognize patterns	Parks require cooperation to stay clean
Abstract Continuity	Imagine improvements	Add recycling bins and community rules

By climbing this ladder, children learn to combine observation with thoughtful decision-making.

Moving Forward

As you continue through the book, remember that understanding systems and thinking ethically are closely connected.

Observation without reflection is incomplete.

Action without understanding can create unintended problems.

But when we combine careful observation with thoughtful reasoning, we become better decision-makers.

Each exercise strengthens your ability to:

- recognize patterns in systems
- predict consequences
- consider ethical responsibilities
- imagine solutions that benefit others

By practicing these skills, you are not only improving comprehension—you are also preparing to become a thoughtful and responsible participant in the systems that shape our world.

And that journey continues in the next chapter, where you will explore how these thinking skills can help prevent mistakes, guide better decisions, and support a successful life.

CHAPTER 4

Preventing "Life Failures" Through Learning

Every day, people make decisions.

Some decisions are small, such as choosing what to eat for breakfast, deciding whether to finish homework before playing, or choosing how to speak to a friend. Other decisions are larger and may affect friendships, learning, health, opportunities, and the future.

Many of these decisions may seem unimportant in the moment. A single choice can feel small, quick, and easy to forget. But over time, small choices often add up. They begin to shape habits, attitudes, and the direction of a person's life.

Most people do not wake up intending to make poor choices. In fact, many problems in life happen simply because people act too quickly without thinking carefully about what might happen next.

Someone might say something hurtful during an argument without thinking about how those words might affect a friend. Another person might ignore schoolwork because it feels difficult at the moment, only to discover later that learning gaps have made future lessons harder. Someone may choose the easiest option again and again without realizing that easy choices in the short term sometimes create harder problems later.

Sometimes mistakes happen because people follow the crowd instead of thinking for themselves. At other times, people rush into decisions because they feel strong emotions such as anger, excitement, fear, or frustration. When emotions take control, people may react before they fully understand the situation.

This chapter introduces a powerful skill that helps people make wiser choices.

That skill is called **foresight**.

Foresight means the ability to imagine possible outcomes before taking action. It is the habit of pausing and asking thoughtful questions, such as:

- What might happen if I do this?
- How could this affect other people?
- Will this choice help or harm my future?
- Are there better options available?
- What problems could this create later?
- What good could come from making a wiser choice now?

When children begin practicing foresight early in life, they build habits that support self-control, responsibility, and confidence.

The visual thinking skills you practiced earlier—observation, inference, thematic understanding, and abstract thinking—now help you do something even more important:

They help you predict consequences and make wiser decisions.

These skills are not just useful for solving puzzles or understanding scenes in a book. They are skills for living. They help children understand not only what they see, but what actions may lead to. They help transform thinking into guidance.

Understanding "Life Failures"

The phrase **"life failure"** may sound serious, but it does not mean that a person has failed as a human being. Everyone makes mistakes. Mistakes are a natural part of learning and growing.

A mistake can become a lesson if a person reflects on it, learns from it, and makes a better choice the next time.

However, certain patterns of behavior can create problems that affect opportunities and well-being over time. These patterns do not usually begin as large disasters. More often, they begin as repeated small choices that slowly build into larger consequences.

Life failures often occur when:

- warning signs are ignored
- actions are taken without thinking about consequences
- Impulsive decisions become habits
- long-term goals are forgotten in favor of short-term comfort
- responsibility is avoided again and again
- reflection does not happen after mistakes are made

For example, imagine a student who consistently avoids practicing difficult subjects such as math or reading. At first, avoiding practice may seem easier than facing the challenge. The student may say, "I'll do it later," or "This is too hard right now."

But over time, the gap in understanding may grow larger.

Later lessons become more confusing, and confidence may begin to decrease. The student may start believing that they are simply "not good" at the subject, even though the real problem was not ability. The real problem was repeated avoidance.

The same pattern can happen in friendships. A person who never apologizes when they hurt others may slowly damage trust. A person who refuses to listen may slowly weaken important relationships. A person who acts unfairly may eventually find that others no longer want to cooperate with them.

The problem did not happen in one moment. It developed slowly through repeated small choices.

This is why foresight is so valuable.

When people learn to pause and imagine possible outcomes, they gain the ability to guide their lives more thoughtfully. They begin to notice that today's small actions often shape tomorrow's opportunities.

Confidence Through Understanding

Many people believe confidence means always feeling certain or never making mistakes.

In reality, true confidence comes from something different.

Confidence grows when people know they can:

- observe a situation carefully
- think about possible outcomes
- make thoughtful decisions
- learn from mistakes
- adapt when things do not go as planned

When children develop these abilities, they feel more capable of facing challenges.

Confidence is not about knowing everything. It is about trusting your ability to think, learn, and improve.

For example, a student who understands that practice strengthens learning may choose to review lessons regularly. Even if a subject is difficult at first, the student knows that improvement will come with effort. This knowledge builds real confidence because it is based on experience, not wishful thinking.

Another student who understands the importance of kindness may choose to support a classmate who feels left out. Over time, that student learns that thoughtful choices can strengthen friendships and create trust.

These decisions may seem small in the moment. But repeated thoughtful choices gradually shape a person's life.

Confidence grows when children see that careful thinking leads to positive outcomes. When they notice that thoughtful preparation reduces stress, that kindness strengthens trust, and that reflection helps improve future decisions, they begin trusting their own ability to handle life responsibly.

The Power of Foresight

Foresight is like having a mental telescope that allows you to look ahead into the future.

You cannot know exactly what will happen, but you can imagine possible outcomes based on the information you observe.

This ability helps people make better choices because it encourages them to think beyond the present moment.

For example:

If you see dark clouds gathering in the sky, you may predict that rain is coming and decide to bring an umbrella.

If you notice that a friend seems upset, you may predict that they need kindness or support.

If you realize that an important assignment is due soon, you may begin preparing early to avoid stress later.

If you see that a playground surface has become slippery after rain, you may predict that someone could fall if people keep running.

Each of these decisions comes from the ability to think ahead.

Foresight uses the same thinking skills developed in the Cognitive Ladder.

Observation helps you notice important details.

Inference helps you predict what might happen next.

Thematic understanding helps you recognize patterns.

Abstract thinking allows you to imagine long-term outcomes and changes over time.

Together, these skills help you pause and think before acting.

That pause is powerful.

Sometimes the difference between a wise decision and a harmful one is simply a moment of thoughtful reflection. A person who pauses has time to choose. A person who never pauses often reacts instead of deciding.

Impulsive Actions vs. Thoughtful Decisions

An **impulsive action** happens quickly, often driven by strong emotion or immediate desire.

Examples might include:

- interrupting someone during an argument

- copying someone else's work instead of learning

- ignoring safety rules

- reacting angrily without listening

- grabbing something because you want it right away

- following others into poor behavior just to fit in

Impulsive decisions may feel satisfying in the moment, but they often create problems later.

A **thoughtful decision**, on the other hand, includes a moment of reflection.

Before acting, a thoughtful person might ask:

- What are the possible outcomes?

- How will this affect others?

- Is this the best choice for the future?

- Am I reacting to emotion or responding with understanding?

- What would happen if everyone did this?

This brief pause allows the brain to move from reaction to careful reasoning.

Learning to pause and think is one of the most valuable habits a person can develop. It strengthens self-control, protects relationships, and reduces preventable mistakes.

Over time, thoughtful decision-making becomes easier because the brain becomes accustomed to considering consequences before acting.

Applying Lessons to Everyday Life

The thinking skills in this book are not meant only for classroom exercises. They are tools that help guide everyday life.

Each day provides opportunities to practice thoughtful decision-making.

At School

Students may notice that completing assignments regularly reduces stress and strengthens understanding. When work is finished on time, learning becomes more enjoyable, and confidence grows.

They also learn the value of cooperation by working together on projects, helping classmates understand difficult lessons, and respecting classroom rules.

A student who studies a little each day often feels calmer during tests than a student who waits until the last minute.

At Home

Helping with responsibilities—such as cleaning, cooking, organizing, or caring for younger siblings—builds trust and cooperation within the family.

Listening carefully during conversations strengthens communication and understanding.

Families function best when people consider how their choices affect one another.

With Friends

Friendships grow stronger when people listen, speak kindly, and respect one another.

When disagreements occur, thoughtful communication can prevent hurt feelings and build stronger relationships. A person who pauses before speaking may avoid saying something harmful that cannot easily be taken back.

In the Community

Respecting shared spaces—parks, libraries, streets, and schools—helps everyone live comfortably together.

Small actions, such as picking up litter, waiting your turn, following rules, or helping others, contribute to healthier communities.

Over time, thoughtful habits become easier to practice.

When good thinking becomes routine, wise decisions become more natural.

Visual Thinking and Real-Life Decisions

Earlier in the book, you practiced studying scenes carefully and asking questions about what might happen next.

The same method can help you understand real-life situations.

Imagine this scene:

A group of children is playing near a river.

One child begins throwing trash into the water.

Pause and think.

Ask yourself:

- What is happening in this scene?
- Who might be affected by this action?
- What might happen if this behavior continues?

By thinking carefully, you might realize that pollution harms animals, plants, and people who rely on clean water.

Fish may become sick. Plants may struggle to grow. Communities may lose an important source of water. The river may no longer be a safe place for recreation or life.

A thoughtful decision might be to encourage proper disposal of trash, explain why the action is harmful, or help clean the area.

This example shows how visual understanding connects to ethical choices.

Seeing clearly often leads to acting responsibly.

The Habit of Reflection

Another powerful thinking skill is **reflection.**

Reflection means taking time to think about experiences and learn from them.

Instead of rushing from one event to the next, reflective thinkers pause and ask questions such as:

- What happened?
- What choices were made?
- What went well?
- What could be improved next time?
- What did I learn from this experience?

Reflection allows people to learn from both successes and mistakes.

If a situation went well, reflection helps identify the habits that contributed to success.

If a mistake occurred, reflection helps identify how to make better choices in the future.

Importantly, reflection is not about blaming yourself or others.

It is about learning and growing.

Every experience becomes an opportunity to become wiser.

Reflection turns life into a classroom.

Practice: Predicting Outcomes and Making Thoughtful Decisions

The following scenarios encourage you to practice foresight and ethical thinking.

Read each situation carefully and consider the possible outcomes.

Scenario 1 – Studying for Success

A student decides to study a little each day before an important exam.

Questions to consider:

- How might this affect the student's confidence?

- What outcome might they experience during the exam?
- How could consistent effort now influence future learning?

Scenario 2 – Words Matter

A student hears a rumor about a classmate and repeats it without checking if it is true.

Questions to consider:

- How could this affect friendships?
- What might happen if the rumor spreads further?
- How could thoughtful communication prevent harm?

Scenario 3 – Helping Hands

A child notices a younger student struggling to carry a stack of books.

Questions to consider:

- What might happen if the child offers help?
- How might the younger student feel?
- How does helping others strengthen a community?

Scenario 4 – Caring for the Environment

A group of children is playing near a river. One child throws trash into the water.

Questions to consider:

- Who might be affected by this action?
- What long-term effects could pollution cause?
- What actions could improve the situation?

Scenario 5 – Fairness in Daily Choices

Two clubs at school meet at the same time, preventing students from attending both.

Questions to consider:

- How might this affect students?
- What changes might allow fair participation?
- Why is fairness important in decision-making?

Each scenario teaches that choices have consequences, and thoughtful reflection can lead to better outcomes.

Learning Today, Shaping Tomorrow

The thinking skills you practice today will influence many decisions in the future.

When children develop foresight, ethical awareness, and self-control, they gain the ability to guide their lives with wisdom.

Small daily decisions accumulate over time.

Habits form.

Opportunities grow.

Relationships strengthen.

Character develops.

Education is not only about memorizing information.

It is about learning **how to think clearly and act responsibly**.

By strengthening your ability to observe, predict, reflect, and choose wisely, you are preparing yourself to build a life guided by understanding and purpose.

And the thoughtful habits you develop today will continue shaping your future for many years to come.

CHAPTER 5

Legacy and Future Thinking

Thinking Beyond Today

Every action we take today can influence tomorrow.

Sometimes the results of our choices appear quickly. If you help someone carry a heavy bag, you may see their gratitude immediately. If you clean your room, the space becomes neat and comfortable right away. If you apologize after hurting a friend's feelings, the relationship may begin to heal.

But many actions do not reveal their results so quickly.

Some choices quietly shape the future in ways that may take months, years, or even generations to fully appear. A person who studies regularly may not notice the benefits right away, but over time, knowledge grows. A community that plants trees today may not see the forest fully grown for many years, yet future generations will enjoy the shade and fresh air those trees provide.

The way people treat one another, the way they care for the environment, the way they solve problems, and the way they use knowledge can influence the future of families, communities, and the planet.

This chapter introduces an important idea called **legacy thinking**.

A legacy is something a person leaves behind that continues to influence others long after the original action has taken place.

When people hear the word "legacy," they often imagine famous leaders, inventors, or historical figures whose names appear in textbooks. They may think about explorers who discovered new lands, scientists who made important discoveries, or leaders who shaped the direction of nations.

But legacy is not limited to famous individuals.

Every person contributes to the future through the choices they make and the habits they practice each day. Even small actions can create ripples that spread far beyond the moment in which they occur.

What Is Legacy?

A **legacy** is the lasting influence of a person's actions, ideas, or contributions.

Sometimes legacy appears in visible ways.

A scientist may invent a new technology that helps people communicate across the world. An architect may design buildings that support communities for many years. A teacher may inspire students who later become innovators, leaders, or problem-solvers.

These examples may seem large, but many legacies grow quietly.

A parent who teaches kindness and responsibility influences how children treat others. Those children may grow up and pass the same values on to their own families.

A student who helps classmates learn creates a culture of cooperation. Over time, that culture can strengthen an entire classroom or school.

A community that protects forests and rivers preserves those environments for future generations. People who live in that community years later will benefit from the clean water and natural beauty that earlier generations chose to protect.

Legacy is not about fame or recognition.

It is about a **positive influence that continues over time**.

Often, legacy grows from small actions repeated consistently. Curiosity, kindness, responsibility, and thoughtful decision-making may seem simple. Yet when practiced every day, these habits gradually shape families, classrooms, neighborhoods, and societies.

When people begin to recognize that their actions contribute to something larger than themselves, they often become more thoughtful about the choices they make.

They begin asking questions such as:

How might my actions affect others?

What kind of example am I setting?

What kind of world am I helping create?

These questions are the beginning of legacy thinking.

The Power of Comprehension

One of the most powerful tools for shaping the future is **understanding**.

When people understand the world deeply, they are better able to improve it. They can see patterns, recognize problems early, and imagine solutions that others may not notice.

Comprehension allows individuals to:

- recognize patterns
- understand cause and effect
- evaluate possible outcomes
- imagine better solutions

Learning is sometimes misunderstood as simply collecting information. A person might memorize facts, definitions, or lists of details without truly understanding how those ideas connect to the real world.

But information alone does not automatically lead to wisdom.

True learning happens when knowledge is connected, examined, and applied thoughtfully.

When young minds practice observing carefully, drawing reasonable inferences, identifying themes, and thinking abstractly about systems, they begin to see the world more clearly.

Instead of viewing events as isolated moments, they recognize patterns that link many experiences together.

For example, a student who studies ecosystems may learn that plants, animals, water, and soil all interact with one another. Later, when that student sees pollution affecting a river, they may immediately understand that the damage could spread through the entire ecosystem.

This deeper level of comprehension prepares people to approach challenges creatively and responsibly.

It allows them to move beyond reacting to problems and begin designing solutions.

The thinking skills developed throughout this book are therefore more than academic tools.

They are foundations for thoughtful leadership, responsible citizenship, and creative problem-solving.

Future Thinking: Imagining Possibilities

Human beings possess an extraordinary ability.

We can imagine possibilities that have not yet happened.

This ability is called **future thinking**.

Future thinking allows people to plan, invent, build, and improve the systems that support human life. It allows engineers to design bridges before they are built, scientists to imagine discoveries that have not yet been made, and communities to plan improvements that will benefit future generations.

When individuals practice future thinking, they begin to notice that the world is constantly shaped by decisions.

Small choices accumulate over time.

These choices gradually create conditions that influence how communities function and how environments change.

Future thinking encourages individuals to step back from the present moment and ask broader questions:

- What might happen if this continues?
- What outcomes could different decisions create?
- Which path leads to the most positive long-term results?

Instead of focusing only on what is easiest today, thoughtful individuals begin considering what will be most beneficial over time.

This habit strengthens patience, responsibility, and careful judgment.

People who practice future thinking often become better planners, problem-solvers, and leaders because they are able to see beyond immediate circumstances.

Connecting Present Choices to Future Outcomes

One of the most important lessons in legacy thinking is that **today's actions become tomorrow's conditions**.

Imagine a forest that people choose to protect.

Trees continue growing.

Animals maintain their habitats.

Clean air and water remain available.

Future generations inherit a healthy environment.

Now imagine the same forest being cleared without careful planning.

Animals lose their homes.

Soil becomes unstable.

Water systems may change.

Future generations inherit environmental challenges.

The difference between these two outcomes begins with the choices made today.

The same principle applies to many parts of life.

Education decisions affect future opportunities.

Community cooperation affects safety and stability.

Environmental protection affects natural resources.

Honesty and responsibility influence trust between people.

When people understand these connections, they begin to recognize the importance of thoughtful decision-making.

They begin to realize that even small actions contribute to larger outcomes.

Shaping Communities Through Understanding

Communities are complex systems made up of many connected parts.

Schools, homes, businesses, parks, technologies, and social relationships all interact with one another. When these parts work together effectively, communities become healthier, safer, and more productive.

When people understand how these systems function, they are better able to improve them.

Knowledge helps individuals recognize challenges that might otherwise go unnoticed.

It also enables them to imagine creative solutions that benefit larger groups of people.

Progress in many areas of society begins with someone who recognizes a problem clearly and imagines a better approach.

Education, science, environmental protection, technology, and public health all advance when thoughtful individuals apply knowledge responsibly.

Understanding systems also helps people recognize the importance of cooperation.

Communities function best when individuals work together with shared goals and mutual respect.

Trust, fairness, and responsibility become essential foundations for long-term progress.

Responsibility for the Future

With knowledge comes responsibility.

When individuals understand how systems work and how decisions influence others, they begin to recognize that their actions carry consequences beyond themselves.

Responsible thinking means considering how choices may affect:

- other people
- shared environments
- future generations

This awareness does not mean people must always make perfect decisions.

No one can predict every outcome or solve every challenge immediately.

Responsibility simply means continuing to learn, reflect, and improve decisions over time.

Thoughtful individuals regularly ask themselves important questions:

- Does this decision help or harm others?
- Will this action improve conditions or create new problems?
- How can I contribute to solutions instead of difficulties?

Children who begin practicing this type of thinking early develop habits that guide them throughout life.

As they grow older, these habits help them approach complex issues with curiosity, patience, and care.

Exercise: Thinking About the Future

Consider the following situations and imagine their long-term effects.

Situation 1 – The School Garden

A group of students starts a garden at their school.

They plant vegetables, flowers, and small trees.

Questions to consider:

- How might this project affect the school community?
- How could students learn from caring for the garden?
- What benefits might future students experience?

The garden may provide food, beauty, and learning opportunities for many years.

Situation 2 – Clean Energy

A city decides to invest in clean energy sources such as solar and wind power.

Questions to consider:

- How might this decision affect the environment over time?
- How could cleaner energy improve air quality?
- What benefits might future generations experience?

Thoughtful planning today can create healthier environments tomorrow.

Situation 3 – Learning Strong Skills

A student develops strong problem-solving, communication, and cooperation skills.

Questions to consider:

- How might these abilities help them later in life?
- How could these skills benefit others?
- What opportunities might this create for their community?

Personal growth can also become part of a larger legacy.

Legacy Learning

The goal of this book is not only to improve comprehension skills.

It is to introduce the idea of **Legacy Learning**.

Legacy Learning means developing knowledge, habits, and wisdom that can benefit both the present and the future.

When children learn to:

- observe carefully
- think critically
- understand systems
- make ethical decisions
- consider long-term consequences

They begin developing the ability to shape their communities and protect the world around them.

Small actions today can create positive changes that continue far into the future.

Helping others, protecting nature, and thinking before acting—these simple habits contribute to a better world.

A Future Shaped by Thoughtful Minds

The future of the world will be shaped by the decisions of people who are learning today.

Children who develop strong thinking skills may become:

- scientists discovering solutions to global challenges
- teachers inspiring future generations
- engineers designing new technologies
- leaders strengthening communities
- artists expressing ideas that inspire change

But regardless of the paths people choose, the ability to think carefully and act responsibly will always remain valuable.

By practicing observation, reasoning, ethical thinking, and foresight, you are strengthening abilities that can guide the future toward cooperation, sustainability, and understanding.

The scenes you explored in this book were more than pictures.

They were opportunities to train your mind to notice connections, imagine possibilities, and make responsible choices.

Every thoughtful decision contributes to a better future.

And the journey begins with one simple habit:

Learning to see the world clearly and thinking carefully about how your actions can help shape it.

A Message to Parents and Teachers

Children are naturally curious. From the moment they begin exploring the world, they observe colors, shapes, movements, sounds, and patterns. Long before they can read written words, they are already learning to interpret the visual and social environments around them.

A child watches how people interact. They notice how objects move, how people respond to one another, and how actions lead to outcomes. These early observations form the foundation of understanding.

This book is built on a simple but powerful principle: **visual comprehension can become the foundation for lifelong thinking skills.**

By encouraging children to observe scenes carefully, ask questions, recognize patterns, and think about consequences, we help them develop cognitive abilities that extend far beyond early reading. Instead of memorizing isolated facts, children begin learning how to interpret complex environments and understand relationships between events.

Observation becomes the starting point for deeper learning.

When children learn to observe carefully, they begin noticing details that others might overlook. They see connections between actions and outcomes. They begin asking thoughtful questions about the world around them.

These questions are the seeds of curiosity.

Curiosity leads to exploration.

Exploration leads to understanding.

Understanding leads to wisdom.

This progression represents the true purpose of education.

The Role of Adults in Developing Thinking Skills

Parents and teachers play an important role in nurturing children's curiosity and guiding their thinking. While children naturally explore their surroundings, adults help transform these observations into meaningful learning experiences.

One of the most effective ways adults can support this process is through **conversation**.

Simple discussions about what children see can strengthen several important abilities:

- attention and focus
- memory and recall
- reasoning and problem-solving
- emotional awareness
- ethical decision-making

Instead of focusing only on correct answers, conversations can encourage deeper thinking.

For example, instead of asking only:

"What do you see?"

You might ask:

- What might happen next?
- Why do you think that is happening?
- How are the people or animals connected?
- What might change if someone made a different choice?
- How might this situation affect others?

Questions like these encourage children to move beyond observation and begin thinking about relationships, causes, consequences, and responsibilities.

This kind of discussion strengthens the **Cognitive Ladder** that forms the foundation of this book.

Children learn to:

1. Observe carefully.
2. Interpret what they see.
3. Understand patterns and themes.
4. Imagine possible futures.

These skills support learning across many subjects, including science, literature, history, and mathematics.

But perhaps even more importantly, they support thoughtful decision-making in everyday life.

Encouraging Curiosity Instead of Memorization

In many educational settings, children are asked to memorize information quickly. While memorization can sometimes be helpful, it is not the same as understanding.

True learning happens when children are encouraged to explore ideas, ask questions, and connect information with real experiences.

When a child asks a question, it is an opportunity for discovery.

Instead of immediately providing answers, adults can encourage further exploration.

For example:

If a child asks why leaves change color in autumn, a teacher or parent might explore the idea together by observing trees, discussing seasons, and connecting the observation to plant biology.

When children learn through exploration, they develop a stronger connection to knowledge. They learn not only **what** something is, but also **why** it happens and **how** it fits into a larger system.

This approach strengthens both comprehension and curiosity.

The Importance of Ethical Thinking

Another important aspect of learning is ethical awareness.

Children naturally observe how people treat one another. They notice fairness, kindness, cooperation, and responsibility.

By encouraging discussions about ethical choices, adults help children develop empathy and moral reasoning.

For example, when discussing a scene where someone helps another person, you might ask:

- Why was that action helpful?

- How might the other person feel?

- What might happen if more people behaved that way?

Similarly, when examining situations involving conflict or unfairness, children can be encouraged to consider alternative actions and possible solutions.

These discussions help children develop the habit of thinking not only about **what they can do**, but also about **what they should do**.

Over time, this awareness becomes part of their decision-making process.

Building Lifelong Thinking Habits

The goal of this book is not simply to improve reading comprehension or visual analysis.

The goal is to help children develop **lifelong thinking habits**.

Children who learn to observe carefully and reflect thoughtfully gain tools that will help them throughout life.

They become better problem-solvers.

They communicate ideas more clearly.

They recognize patterns in complex situations.

They understand that actions have consequences.

They learn to pause before reacting.

These habits prepare children for challenges they will encounter in school, relationships, careers, and communities.

Education becomes more than a process of learning information.

It becomes a way of developing thoughtful, capable individuals.

Conclusion

Learning to Read the World

Throughout this book, you have practiced an important skill: **learning to read the world before reading words**.

Many traditional approaches to learning begin with memorization. Students are often asked to remember definitions, formulas, and explanations before they fully understand how those ideas connect to real life. While memorizing information can sometimes be useful, it does not always help people understand how the world truly works.

This book followed a different path.

Instead of beginning with written text and long explanations, your learning journey began with **observation**. You looked carefully at scenes from nature, cities, communities, and everyday life. By examining these scenes thoughtfully, you trained your mind to notice details, recognize patterns, and ask meaningful questions.

This approach helps the brain learn in a powerful way.

When you observe carefully, your mind begins connecting pieces of information together. You start noticing relationships between objects, people, and environments. Over time, these connections help you understand not only **what is happening**, but also **why it is happening** and **what might happen next**.

This kind of learning transforms simple looking into thoughtful understanding.

Instead of quickly glancing at the world around you, you begin to study it. You notice movement, interactions, and patterns that may have been invisible before. Curiosity grows stronger, and questions naturally begin to appear in your mind.

These thinking habits form a powerful foundation for understanding the world.

The Thinking Skills You Developed

Throughout the book, you practiced several important thinking abilities. Each skill strengthens the others and helps your mind become more capable of understanding complex situations.

Observation

Observation means noticing details carefully and paying attention to what is happening around you.

Strong observers see more than just the obvious. They recognize patterns, relationships, and changes that others might overlook. A careful observer might notice how shadows move throughout the day, how animals behave in different environments, or how people cooperate to complete tasks.

Observation is the starting point for discovery.

Many important discoveries throughout history began when someone noticed something interesting and asked a question about it. By training yourself to observe carefully, you are developing the same skill used by scientists, explorers, inventors, and artists.

Observation strengthens patience, focus, and curiosity.

Inference

Inference involves using evidence to make thoughtful predictions or explanations.
When you infer, you look at clues and think carefully about what those clues might mean. Instead of guessing randomly, you use what you observe to build logical ideas about what may happen next.

You may ask questions such as:

- What might happen next?

- Why is this happening?

- What clues help explain this situation?

Inference helps you connect what you see with what you know. It allows you to think ahead and anticipate outcomes. This skill is extremely valuable because it helps people solve problems and make wiser decisions.

Thematic Understanding

Thematic understanding involves recognizing the larger ideas or messages within a scene.

Sometimes a situation communicates more than what appears on the surface. A picture showing people helping each other might reveal themes of cooperation and kindness. A scene showing pollution or environmental damage might highlight the importance of responsibility and care for nature.

Thematic thinking helps connect individual observations to broader meaning.

It encourages you to think about what situations represent and why they matter. This ability allows people to learn lessons from experiences and apply those lessons in new situations.

Abstract Thinking

Abstract thinking allows you to consider systems, relationships, and possibilities that extend beyond the immediate moment.

Instead of focusing only on what you can see directly, abstract thinking asks deeper questions, such as:

- How might this system change over time?
- What would happen if one part of the system changed?
- How do different parts influence one another?

This type of thinking allows people to imagine possibilities that have not yet happened. It supports creativity, innovation, and long-term planning.

Abstract thinking helps people design new technologies, improve communities, and solve complex challenges.

Foresight

Foresight is the ability to imagine possible outcomes before taking action.

It encourages people to pause and think carefully about consequences. Instead of acting quickly without reflection, individuals who practice foresight consider how their choices might affect others, their environment, and their future opportunities.

Foresight strengthens responsibility and helps individuals avoid many preventable problems.

It transforms thinking into guidance for making wiser decisions.

Learning Continues Beyond the Book

Although this book has reached its final pages, your learning journey is only beginning.

The world around you is filled with scenes waiting to be explored and understood.

A walk through a park reveals ecosystems where plants, animals, water, and sunlight interact. A city street demonstrates complex systems of transportation, communication, and cooperation. A classroom shows how knowledge grows through curiosity, effort, and collaboration.

Even ordinary moments can become powerful learning experiences when you observe them carefully.

A conversation between friends can teach you about empathy and communication. A community project can teach you about teamwork and responsibility. A change in the weather can teach you about natural systems and environmental patterns.

When you learn to observe deeply, **every place becomes a classroom**.

Every situation becomes an opportunity to learn.

The thinking skills you practiced in this book—observation, inference, thematic understanding, abstract thinking, and foresight—are not limited to exercises on a page. They are lifelong tools that help you understand the world, solve problems, and make thoughtful decisions.

As you continue growing and exploring, these skills will guide your curiosity and strengthen your ability to contribute positively to the communities and environments around you.

Learning to read the world is one of the most valuable abilities you can develop.

Because when you truly learn to see, understand, and think carefully about what surrounds you, the world becomes not only a place to live— but also a place full of lessons, discoveries, and possibilities waiting to unfold.

The Reader's Promise

Every great journey begins with learning how to see.

By reading this book, you have practiced looking carefully at the world around you. You have learned how to notice details, recognize patterns, think about consequences, and imagine what might happen next. These skills help transform simple observation into meaningful understanding.

But learning does not stop here.

In fact, this book is only the beginning of a much larger journey. The world around you is full of scenes waiting to be explored: forests, cities, oceans, classrooms, neighborhoods, and the many people you meet every day. Each place and situation contains connections, challenges, and opportunities to learn.

A tree growing in a park may teach you about ecosystems and balance.

A busy street may teach you about cooperation and shared responsibility.

A conversation with a friend may teach you about kindness and understanding.

When you observe the world carefully, even ordinary moments can become powerful lessons.

As you continue growing and learning, remember these important ideas:

• **Observe carefully.**

Take time to notice details that others might overlook.

• **Think before acting.**

Pause and consider how your choices may affect others and the future.

• **Ask thoughtful questions.**

Curiosity is the starting point of discovery and understanding.

• Consider how your actions affect others.

Every decision can influence people, communities, and the environment.

• Imagine the future you want to help create.

Thoughtful choices today can shape a better tomorrow.

When you practice these habits, you are doing more than learning—you are preparing yourself to make wise decisions and positive changes in the world.

The skills you are developing now will help you understand complex problems, work cooperatively with others, and contribute solutions that improve communities and protect the planet.

This is the beginning of **Legacy Learning**, the idea that knowledge, wisdom, and responsibility can grow from one generation to the next.

And it begins with you.

You have the ability to observe carefully, think deeply, and make decisions that influence the world around you. Every thoughtful action you take becomes part of the future that others will experience.

To remind yourself of this responsibility and opportunity, you can make a simple promise:

Today, I promise to:

Observe the world carefully.

Think deeply about what I see.

Make choices that help others.

Learn from every experience.

And use my understanding to build a better future.

Because learning to read the world is the first step toward helping the world grow.

About Legacy Learning

The ultimate goal of this book is not only to improve comprehension but also to cultivate **Legacy Learning**.

Legacy Learning means developing knowledge, habits, and wisdom that benefit both the present and future generations. It encourages individuals to think beyond immediate results and consider the long-term effects of their actions.

When children learn to:

- observe carefully
- think critically
- understand systems
- make ethical decisions
- consider long-term consequences

They begin developing the ability to shape their communities and protect the world around them.

Small actions today—helping others, protecting nature, thinking before acting, and learning from experience—can create positive changes that continue far into the future.

By learning to read the world, children prepare themselves to become thoughtful leaders, responsible citizens, and creative problem-solvers.

The journey of understanding always begins with curiosity.

Curiosity leads to discovery, growth, and the possibility of building a better world for everyone.